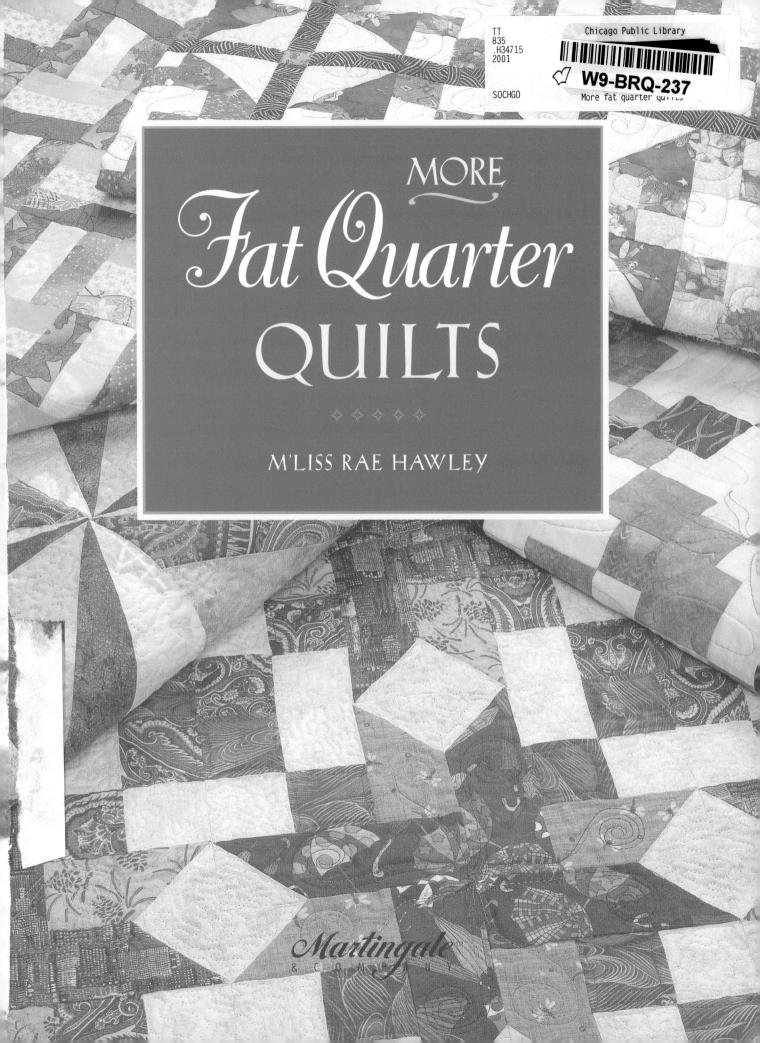

TT
835
.H34715
2001

SOCHGO

Chicago Public Library

W9-BRQ-237

More fat quarter quilts

MORE
Fat Quarter
QUILTS

✦ ✦ ✦ ✦ ✦

M'LISS RAE HAWLEY

Martingale
& COMPANY

More Fat Quarter Quilts
© 2001 by M'Liss Rae Hawley

That Patchwork Place® is an imprint
of Martingale & Company™.

Martingale & Company
20205 144th Ave. NE
Woodinville, WA 98072-8478
www.martingale-pub.com

Credits
President: Nancy J. Martin
CEO: Daniel J. Martin
Publisher: Jane Hamada
Editorial Director: Mary V. Green
Managing Editor: Tina Cook
Technical Editor: Laurie Baker
Copy Editor: Karen Koll
Design and Production Manager: Stan Green
Illustrator: Robin Strobel
Cover Designer: Stan Green
Text Designer: Regina Girard
Photographer: Brent Kane

No part of this product may be reproduced in any form, unless otherwise stated, in which case reproduction is limited to the use of the purchaser. The written instructions, photographs, designs, projects, and patterns are intended for the personal, noncommercial use of the retail purchaser and are under federal copyright laws; they are not to be reproduced by any electronic, mechanical, or other means, including informational storage or retrieval systems, for commercial use. Permission is granted to photocopy patterns for the personal use of the retail purchaser.

The information in this book is presented in good faith, but no warranty is given nor results guaranteed. Since Martingale & Company has no control over choice of materials or procedures, the company assumes no responsibility for the use of this information.

Printed in China
06 05 04 03 02 01   8 7 6 5 4 3 2 1

Library of Congress Cataloging-in-Publication Data
Hawley, M'Liss Rae
    More fat quarter quilts / M'Liss Rae Hawley.
        p. cm.
    ISBN 1-56477-391-4
    1. Patchwork—Patterns. 2. Quilting—Patterns. I. Title.

TT835 .H34715 2001
746.46'041—dc21   2001044169

Mission Statement
We are dedicated to providing quality products and service by working together to inspire creativity and to enrich the lives we touch.

SOC

R0174505613

✧ Dedication ✧

I would like to dedicate this book to my parents, Josephine Walsh and Kenneth Ray Frandsen. They have encouraged and inspired my lifelong love affair with textiles, making many trips to fabric stores, sewing lessons, fashion shows, museums, and art galleries when I was younger, plus making the financial commitment of six years of college.

✧ Acknowledgments ✧

My sister, Erin Rae Frandsen, has been an unwavering supporter of my many endeavors in the wonderful world of textiles. She is always available to cut more fabric, help bind yet another quilt, and deliver or pick up quilts from Martingale. Thank you, Erin!

I am extremely grateful for the generosity of Mr. B., owner of Benartex Inc. Many of my quilts in this book were made with fabrics from his company. He is passionate about the quality of his fabric, a true quilter's friend, and a fine host! Thanks also to David Lochner and the rest of the crew.

Beth Hayes, editor of *McCall's Quilting*, has been steadfast in her acknowledgment and encouragement of my work. I most gratefully thank her for this.

Sulky of America continues to create new and wonderful threads for quilters. Fred Drexler was especially generous in providing me with rayon thread for the Embroidery Block quilts. His enthusiasm for the industry is wonderful!

American & Efird, Inc., the exclusive distributor to the United States for Mettler threads, has also contributed to this endeavor. Mettler cotton threads are unsurpassed in quality and color range! A special thank-you to Marci Brier.

Quilters Dream Cotton keeps on producing a variety of great battings. Kathy Thompson and Jo Barrow are always helpful in finding just the right batting for each and every project. Thank you so much!

Also, I offer a thank-you to Judy Martin, owner of Island Fabrics, Freeland, Washington, for her technical assistance with the Embroidery block.

I would like to acknowledge all of my students worldwide, especially the ones that live on Whidbey Island or travel to the island to take classes from me. These women are dedicated to and passionate about quilting. They have put many thoughtful hours into fabric selection, classes, and the most wonderful of all, finishing their projects! This book is a testament to their devotion. Thank you so much!

CHICAGO PUBLIC LIBRARY
SOUTH CHICAGO BRANCH
9055 S. HOUSTON AVE. 606.

Contents

Introduction

✧ 7 ✧

General Directions

✧ 9 ✧

✧ ✧ ✧ ✧ ✧

Projects

Gallery of Quilts
✧ 51 ✧

Quilt Finishing
✧ 71 ✧

About the Author
✧ 79 ✧

✧ ✧ ✧ ✧ ✧

Introduction

✧ ✧ ✧ ✧ ✧

Our infatuation with fat quarters continues. We love and adore them! Shops are uncanny in their ability to select the exact six fabrics we want to possess. Featuring everything from new fabric lines, seasonal collections, holiday themes, ethnic subjects, and background assortments, they fold them, wrap them, and even braid them into a dizzying array of enticing, beckoning bundles. Just six 18" x 21" pieces of fabric—fat quarters for the soul.

Fortunately, feeding our addiction has never been easier. A packet of pleasure is just a phone call or mouse click away thanks to mail-order catalogs and Internet shopping. And if you cannot find just the right preassembled packet for the quilt you are making, you can assemble your own. Whether you start with a favorite fabric already in your stash or start from scratch at the fabric store, the do-it-yourself approach is always an option.

When you are ready to undo the package of sweetly wrapped fabrics, you will find that using your fat quarters is just as easy as buying them. *More Fat Quarter Quilts* is my second book on the topic. *Fat Quarter Quilts*, my first book, features eight quilt patterns, all fast and fun! This book also features eight fast-and-fun patterns but with a higher degree of difficulty and interest than those in the first book. For example, Triple Rail on Point is set on point. The Prairie Queen blocks are separated by sashing strips with corner squares. The Embroidery block offers the opportunity to include machine embroidery.

If this is your first fat-quarter book and you are a beginner, consider making the Bargello pattern first. It is the easiest in the book and offers tremendous possibility for creativity. Strait of Georgia is a beginner's dream. It is also an easy block, and almost any color combination or theme works. Triple Rail on Point offers a simple block, but putting the blocks on point makes it more of a challenge.

If size, rather than simplicity, is an issue, Z Star is a great size for a wall hanging, while Prairie Queen is almost bed size. The rest of the projects can be used as baby quilts, picnic throws, tablecloths, or TV blankets. If you want to enlarge the pattern, buy two fat-quarter packets and double the size of the quilt. Or, in the case of Bargello, just add an additional fat quarter and remember to purchase extra background and border fabric.

The formula for great fat-quarter quilts is the same as it was in *Fat Quarter Quilts*:
1. Choose a quilt pattern.
2. Buy your favorite packet of six fat quarters.
3. Pick out a background fabric.
4. Select one or more border fabrics.

If you are a quilter with an in-home collection of fat quarters that aren't assembled into neat little packages, your formula is altered only slightly. Begin with a concept—an idea, be it a color, season, or an event to commemorate. Now, select six fat quarters. It is that easy! The rest of the formula is the same. I hope the quilts in this book will inspire you to make "more fat-quarter quilts"!

More Fat Quarter Quilts comes with the same warning as *Fat Quarter Quilts:* This is an addictive pattern of behavior. Proceed with caution!

General Directions

✦ ✦ ✦ ✦

Supplies

To make the projects in this book, you will need the following supplies:

✦ 100 percent–cotton fabric (a packet of six fat quarters, one or more background fabrics, one or more border fabrics, and backing and binding fabrics)

✦ 100 percent–cotton thread in a neutral color

✦ Batting

✦ Fabric scissors

✦ Glass-head silk pins

✦ Rotary cutting equipment, including

✦ Rotary cutter

✦ Cutting mat

✦ 6" x 24" acrylic ruler

✦ Ruler grips. These self-adhesive tabs are available in plastic, sandpaper, and felt. Apply them to the bottom of your rulers to keep the rulers from slipping while you cut.

✦ Seam ripper

✦ A sewing machine in good working order. A ¼" presser foot helps keep your piecing accurate. Check your sewing-machine manual for the right foot for your machine.

Depending on the project, you might also need the following supplies:

✦ 6" Bias Square® ruler

✦ Embroidery card(s). An embroidery card is a disk containing a collection of digital designs. Embroidery cards are used in special embroidery sewing machines.

✦ Embroidery threads

✦ Fabric stabilizer (refer to "Machine-Embroidery Tips" on page 21)

✦ Foundation paper

Fat-Quarter Packets

Technically, a fat quarter should measure 18" x 21". Practically, when you examine a packet of fat quarters, you may notice slight discrepancies in size. There are several possible reasons for this. While most fabrics are about 42" wide, some manufacturers' fabrics are slightly wider or narrower. Also, the selvage (which includes the fabric identification) takes up some of the width, which means the amount of useable fat quarter will be slightly narrower than 21".

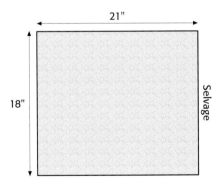

Another variable is the actual cut dimensions. While a perfectly cut fat quarter measures 18" x 21", some shops consistently cut theirs slightly smaller or larger.

I advocate prewashing (see "Preparing Your

Fabrics" on page 12), which will further alter the size of your fat quarters. Laundering often shrinks fabric slightly, and the washing machine can really fray small pieces of fabric.

Because of all the size variables for fat quarters, the patterns in this book are based on fat quarters that are 17" x 20" after prewashing. My advice is to measure all your fat quarters after you wash them and before you cut into them. If any piece of fabric measures less than 17" x 20", you will need an additional fat quarter of that fabric. You may also choose to substitute a different fat quarter.

Depending on the useable size of your fat quarters, you may be able to make more or fewer blocks than the directions call for. That is why when you look at the photos in "Gallery of Quilts" (page 51) you see quilts that are different sizes but made from the same design. The quilters made do with what they had.

✧ Tip ✧

If your local fabric store does not sell fat quarters, buy half-yard pieces. Cut the fabric along the fold to get two fat quarters! Trade with a friend, or stash one fat quarter for another quilt.

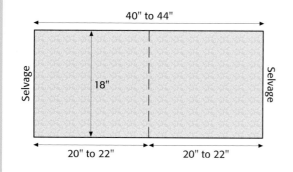

You will cut strips from the 20" length of the fat quarter for all of the patterns except Island Star. For that pattern, you will cut strips along the 17" width.

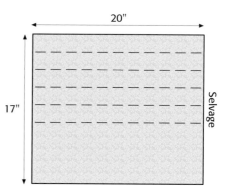

Cutting strips for most quilts

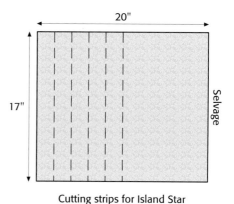

Cutting strips for Island Star

Choosing the Right Fabrics

Fat-quarter packets are available in such tremendous variety that making choices can be overwhelming. I am often asked, "Which comes first, the quilt pattern or the fabric?" I recommend that you select the quilt pattern before you pick the fabric. It is easier to find the appropriate fat-quarter packet, background, and border fabric once you know what you intend to make. On the other hand, if you fall in love with a wonderful theme fabric, buy it! My rule of thumb is to purchase two yards. From that amount, you will be able to cut a fat quarter and all the border strips for any of the quilts in this book.

Fat-quarter bundles are enticing, no matter how they're put together.

Many of the quilts in this book are successful because of the differences in color value in the fabrics. Value is the relative lightness or darkness of a color. I am sure my students are really tired of hearing me harp on this, but value is crucial to a successful end product. Even if you make a monochromatic quilt (a one-color quilt), the difference in value between the fabrics is what makes the quilt work. If you decide to make a monochromatic quilt, consider Bargello for your pattern.

In addition to value, the scale and the variety of the prints you use can also make your work more interesting. Take for example "Galactic Longitude" on page 28. In it, I used all kinds of star fabrics in just about every color possible: little stars, medium stars, big stars, funky stars, traditional stars, shooting stars, and stylized stars. I kept a tight theme, paid attention to value and placement, and had fun.

Once you have chosen a fat-quarter packet, it is time to consider the background fabric. Should it be light or dark? A solid or a print? By studying the quilts in each chapter, you can identify the combinations that appeal to you. What is the value and scale of the background fabric in a quilt you like? Also, consider the end use of your quilt. You might want a bright background for a baby quilt or a dark background for a tablecloth.

I think a quilt's background is as important as its foreground. You should love it! I tend to use yellow and gold as my primary background colors, calling them my "neutrals."

Your next step is to select the border fabric or fabrics. Most quilt shops make fat-quarter packets from newly arrived fabrics. This means the fabrics in the packet are usually still available on the bolt. Repeating one of the fat-quarter fabrics in the border is an easy and sure way to finish your quilt, as I did in my Strait of Georgia quilt, "Tidal Pool" (page 39). If the fabric you want is unavailable, consider one of the following options:

- ✦ Take the darkest color in the fat-quarter packet and choose a fabric that is a little darker.

- ✦ If your fat quarters follow a theme—say, African prints—find a print that works with the theme.

- ✦ If your packet includes a range of colors and patterns, select a floral or paisley print that ties them all together. See "Outdoorsman" on page 54 for an example.

The final step is to choose the binding fabric. Traditionally, the binding is the darkest fabric in the quilt or the same fabric as that used in the outer border. Now that you know this rule, you have permission to do whatever you want. I like to continue the theme of the outer border in the binding. For instance, if I used a floral print for the outer border, I use the same or another floral for the binding. On the Island Star quilt "Best of the Northwest" (page 24), I used a coffee-bean fabric that has almost the same color value as the paisley border. The value was of secondary importance to the theme of the fabric. The coffee beans were too good to pass up!

For help selecting fabrics for the quilts in this book, consult the "Fat-Quarter Adviser" in the directions for each quilt.

Preparing Your Fabrics

When I bring fabric home, anything less than ½ yard goes into the bathroom. I wash it by hand with a liquid detergent (or more likely, my daughter, Adrienne, does!) and hang it to dry. Larger pieces go directly to the laundry room,

where I separate them into light and dark piles. I wash each pile separately. When I am ready to wash the fabrics, I place the pile of fabric in the washing machine, run the water, and check to see if the colors run. If not, I continue with the wash cycle. If the fabrics bleed, I keep rinsing them until the water runs clear and then continue with the wash cycle.

I press all of my fabrics (actually, my husband, Michael, does the pressing) and then I square them up. If the piece is at least 1½" larger than a fat quarter, I cut off a 1½" strip. My plan is to someday make a Log Cabin quilt containing my entire textile history.

Rotary Cutting

Rotary cutting is covered in many quilting books, some of which you probably already have on your shelf, so we will not go into detail here. The basic procedures are the same whether you are cutting fat quarters or full-length yardage. Before cutting strips from the fabric, you must first square up the edges.

Lay a fat quarter on your cutting mat. Place a 6" x 24" ruler on the right-hand side of the fabric so it is perpendicular to the selvage, aligning the end of the ruler so it is flush with the selvage edge. Cut along the right edge of the ruler. Turn the fat quarter so the edge opposite the straightened edge is now on the right-hand side. Straighten this edge in the same manner.

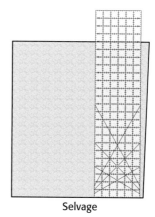

Selvage

Align ruler edge with selvage.

Having established two straight edges, you are ready to begin cutting strips. Occasionally, your fat quarter will need to be squared up after two or three cuts. Repeat the squaring-up process on the edge you are cutting from, and resume cutting.

Paper-Piecing Guidelines

Two of the patterns in this book—Longitude (page 28) and Z Star (page 46)—use paper-piecing methods to stitch blocks together. If you have never paper pieced, don't be intimidated by the technique. It is an easy and accurate method for piecing, and the instructions for each quilt will walk you through the specifics. For both quilts, keep the following in mind when paper piecing:

✦ Trace the pattern in the book onto a foundation material to provide stability for sewing and piecing. There are several products marketed specifically for this purpose, but newsprint, vellum, and tracing paper are also options. Whatever product you choose, be sure you can see through it well enough to place the fabric pieces, and be sure you can tear away the foundation material easily.

✦ The patterns do not include seam allowances, so be sure to extend the fabric pieces at least ⅜" beyond the outer lines. You will trim away any excess when you square up the block.

✦ The patterns are a mirror image of the finished block.

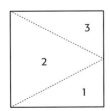
Foundation pattern

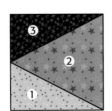
Finished block

✦ Position the foundation with the marked side up. Add the fabric pieces to the unmarked side of the foundation.

✦ Use a stitch length of approximately 10 stitches per inch.

✦ Be sure the fabric pieces extend no less than ¼" and no more than ½" beyond the stitching line. Because you are working with a limited amount of fabric, you must not be too generous with the amount you extend beyond the intended ¼" seam allowance. Hold the foundation and the fabric strips up to a light source to help you position the strips.

✦ Stitch on the marked side of the foundation, beginning and ending with a backstitch ¼" from the edge of the pattern.

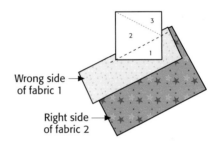

Wrong side of fabric 1

Right side of fabric 2

Stitch with paper on top.

✦ Fold back the paper on the stitched line after each new piece is added. Trim the seam allowances to ¼". Gently press the seam flat to help set the stitches before pressing the seam allowances to one side.

Trim and press.

✦ Tear away the foundation only after the block has been stitched to another block or border strip. The fabrics have been stitched to the foundation with no real concern for grain line, so the edges can readily stretch or become distorted. One easy method for removing the paper is to spray the paper with a fine mist of water. Use a seam ripper to nudge the damp paper gently away from the seam.

Bargello

Bargello: BOW WOW CHOW MEIN by M'Liss Rae Hawley,
2000, Freeland, Washington; quilted by Barbara Dau.

*B*argello is a wonderful traditional needle-point style that has been adapted to other mediums, including quilting. This easy pattern has movement, gives a fabulous impression, and is a great way to showcase luscious fabrics.

✧ ✧ ✧

Fat-Quarter Adviser

The best way to begin is to select your color family or theme fabric. Next, assemble the fabrics by value from light to dark.

This fat-quarter quilt requires a packet of 6 fat quarters, 1 additional fat quarter, and 2 background fabrics. For the upper background fabric, choose a fabric that is close in value to your medium-value fat-quarter fabrics. The lower background fabric should be darker than your darkest fat-quarter fabric.

"Bow Wow Chow Mein" began with the border fabric. It nearly jumped off the shelf, screaming to be made into this pattern! I then chose my fat-quarter fabrics, pulling colors from the border fabric, and arranged them in value from light to dark. You can see from this example how all the fabrics need to work with each other.

Finished Quilt: 61" x 55¼"

Materials

All yardage is based on 42"-wide fabric unless otherwise stated.

1 packet of 6 fat quarters for bargello strips
1 additional coordinating fat quarter for bargello strips
1 yd. coordinating medium color for upper background
1 yd. coordinating dark color for lower background
⅜ yd. for inner border
1⅛ yds. for outer border*
4 yds. for backing
⅝ yd. for binding
Twin-size batting (72" x 90")

Additional yardage may be required if you choose a directional print or one with large motifs. Often, a print with large motifs will look better if it is cut wider than the 7" called for in the cutting directions. The outer-border strips on "Bow Wow Chow Mein" were cut at different widths to take advantage of the interesting and uneven pattern on the fabric.

Cutting

Cut along the 20" length of the fat quarters.

From *each* of the 7 fat quarters, cut:
  6 strips, each 2¼" x 20"

From *each* of the 2 background fabrics, cut:
  2 strips, each 15" x 42". Crosscut to make 3 strips, each 15" x 20".

From the inner-border fabric, cut:
  5 strips, each 1¾" x 42"

From the outer-border fabric, cut:
  5 strips, each 7" x 42"

From the binding fabric, cut:
  6 strips, each 3" x 42"

Assembling the Quilt Top

1. Arrange 1 strip from each of the 7 fat quarters in order from light to dark as shown to make a strip set. With right sides together, pin and sew the strips together. Press the seams toward the darkest strip. Make 6 identical strip sets.

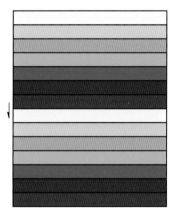

Make 6.

2. Stitch the strip sets together into pairs as shown. Make 3.

Make 3.

3. Stitch a dark background strip to the bottom (darkest fabric) of each strip-set pair. Stitch a medium background strip to the top (lightest fabric) of each strip-set pair. Press the seams toward the dark background fabric (shown top right).

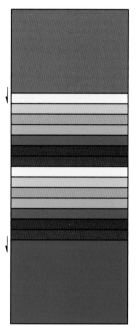

Make 3.

4. To make the strip sets narrow enough to cut with the 6" x 24" ruler, carefully fold the background strips of each strip-set unit so the raw edges of the background fabrics meet. Fold the unit together once more, following the seam allowance of 1 fat-quarter strip.

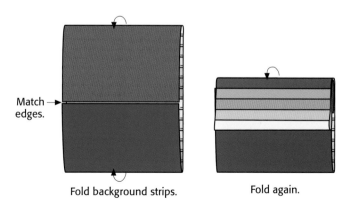

Match edges.

Fold background strips.

Fold again.

5. Crosscut the different strip sets to yield the following total number of strips:

Number of strips	Strip width
1	3¼"
2	3"
3	2¾"
2	2½"
4	2¼"
5	2"
4	1¾"
6	1½"

◇ *Tip* ◇

Group corresponding strip lengths and label each group with the appropriate width.

6. Refer to the illustration below to stitch the strips together. Use the correct-width strip and stagger it up or down 1 segment from the previous segment as shown. At this point, all of the seams are facing in the same direction. Before stitching the rows together, pin the seams for the strips in every other row so they oppose the seams in the previous row. When you have stitched together all the rows, press the vertical seams in one direction and the horizontal seams as pinned.

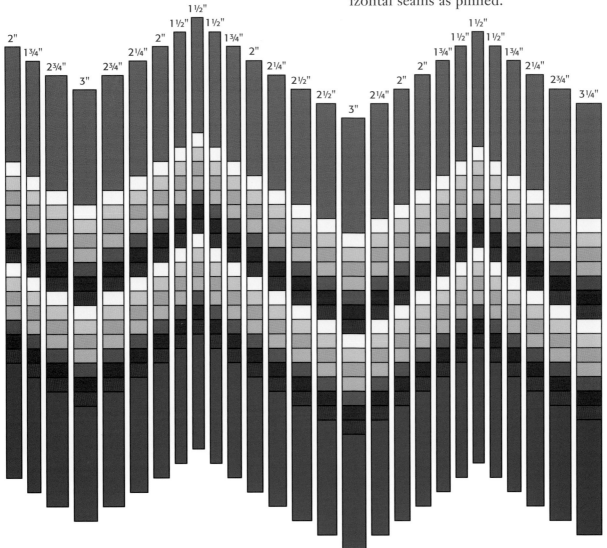

7. Measure from the last fat-quarter segment of each strip into the background piece the amount shown. Make a mark across the strip at the point measured. When you have measured all of the strips, the lines should connect, and each strip should be the same length. Trim across the marked line to square up the quilt.

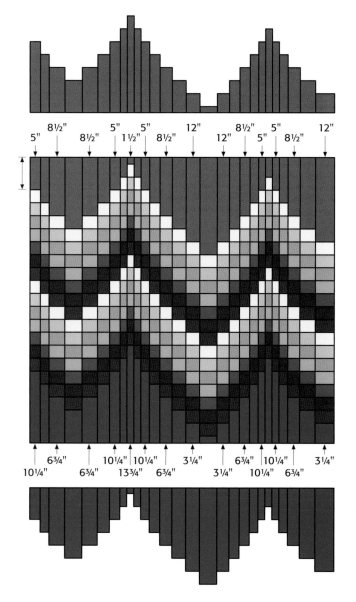

8. Staystitch ¼" from the quilt edges.
9. Referring to "Adding Borders" on pages 71–72, sew the inner border to the top and bottom of the quilt top, and then to the sides, piecing as necessary. Press the seams toward the border. Repeat for the outer border.

Finishing the Quilt

Refer to "Quilt Finishing" on pages 71–78.

1. Layer the quilt top with batting and backing; baste.
2. Quilt as desired.
3. Bind the edges of the quilt.
4. Add a hanging sleeve and label if desired.

The quilted images, inspired by the border fabric, include Chinese lanterns and signs, a garbage can, buildings, and mountains. Rayon thread was used for quilting.

Embroidery Block: CELESTIAL DREAMS by M'Liss Rae Hawley, 1999,
Freeland, Washington; quilted by M'Liss Rae Hawley and Barbara Dau.

✧ ✧ ✧

As a machine-embroidery enthusiast, I wanted to incorporate embroidery with an interesting quilt block. The resulting block consists of the embroidered center square, four half-square-triangle units, and four two-patch segments. The color placement is asymmetrical, which makes the block look more complicated and exciting. I had so much fun with this quilt design that I made five quilts with it. This totaled almost two hundred hours of machine embroidering!

The center block is cut large, so it will fit into the embroidery hoop, and then trimmed. When you are selecting embroidery designs, choose motifs that are no wider than 4½" so they will fit within the trimmed square.

This block can also be made without using a machine-embroidered motif in the center square. Just substitute a square of theme fabric, an appliqué, a hand-embroidered motif, a photo transfer, or a beaded design for the embroidery.

✧ ✧ ✧

Fat-Quarter Adviser

An Embroidery Block quilt is made up of 3 different color combinations of the same block. To choose the fabric combinations, divide the 6 fat quarters into pairs. You can select the pairs based on color family or value, but the best combinations are ones that use a light fabric and a medium-to-dark fabric. When you are finished selecting the combinations, label the pairs 1–3.

After you select the color combinations and before you piece the block, determine the fabric placement within the blocks. I suggest that similar colors or values be positioned in the same location in each block. For an example, look at the position of the green fabrics in "Outdoorsman" on page 54. Each green is in the same position in all 3 of the color combinations. To make the placement easier, refer to the illustrations at right to make a block diagram and a worksheet grid. The block diagram will help you determine how the components in each block will be arranged and the worksheet grid will help you decide the arrangement of all the finished blocks.

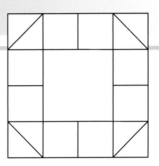

Embroidery Block

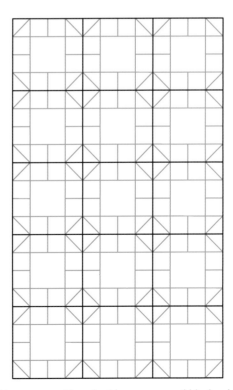

Fill in squares with embroidery names and block colors.

Finished Quilt: 40½" x 58½"
Finished Block: 9"

Materials

All yardage is based on 42"-wide fabric unless otherwise stated.

1¼ yds. for background
1 packet of 6 fat quarters for blocks
¼ yd. for inner border
⅞ yd. for outer border
3 yds. for backing
⅝ yd. for binding
Twin-size batting (72" x 90")
Fabric stabilizer (refer to "Machine-
    Embroidery Tips" at right)
Embroidery card(s) of your choice
Embroidery threads in a variety of colors

Cutting

Cut along the 20" length of the fat quarters.

From the background fabric, cut:

4 strips, each 9½" x 42". Crosscut to make 15 squares, each 9½" x 9½".*

From *each* fat quarter, cut:

2 strips, each 3⅛" x 20". Crosscut to make 10 squares, each 3⅛" x 3⅛"; cut each square in half once diagonally to make 20 triangles.

3 strips, each 2¾" x 20"

From the inner-border fabric, cut:

4 strips, each 1¼" x 42"

From the outer-border fabric, cut:

4 strips, each 6½" x 42"

From the binding fabric, cut:

5 strips, each 3" x 42"

*Adjust the size of the square as needed to fit your embroidery hoop.

Machine-Embroidery Tips

◆ Preshrink the fabric you are using as the background for the embroidery designs.

◆ Use a new needle. Some of the designs have 6,000 to 10,000 stitches per design. When the needle becomes dull, the design can become distorted.

◆ Use a lightweight bobbin thread, such as Madeira's Bobbinfil, a 100 percent–polyester, 70-weight thread. Choose white or black, depending on the color of the background fabric. It is also efficient to pre-wind several bobbins.

◆ There are many different types of fabric stabilizers. I use a tear-away stabilizer under the fabric when I machine embroider, but I often find that a stabilizer placed on top of the fabric produces a more satisfactory end result. I like to use liquid stabilizer if I'm using a white fabric for the background. If you find that you need more stability to keep the fabric from puckering, try a water-soluble or heat-soluble stabilizer.

◆ Make sure the stabilized fabric is in the hoop tightly. This keeps the fabric from moving, which is important when working with compact designs.

◆ If your design is outline stitched, use polyester embroidery thread for the outline stitching. It is strong and does not break as often as other types of thread.

◆ Stitch out a test of the desired embroidery design. Use the background fabric and the threads and stabilizer product you intend to use for the project. This will show you if the thread tension is correct, if the thread coverage is sufficient, and the actual look of the embroidered design on the background fabric. Make adjustments if necessary. Use any embroidered designs that are not quite perfect as labels or incorporate them into the backing.

Assembling the Quilt Top

1. To make the embroidered center squares, follow the manufacturer's instructions to stabilize each 9½" background square and embroider the desired motif. Trim the embroidered squares to 5". You do not have to cut the squares on grain if off grain presents a better overall look.

✧ Tip ✧

To select the best way to trim the embroidered square, use a 5" ruler or tape off all but a 5" square of a larger ruler.

2. To make the half-square-triangle units, group the triangles into pairs according to the predetermined color combinations. You should have 20 pairs of triangles in each color combination (60 total). Stitch the triangles together along the long edges. Press the seams toward the darker fabric.

Make 20 of each color combination (60 total).

3. To make the two-patch segments, group the 2¾" x 20" fat-quarter strips into pairs according to the predetermined color combinations. You should have 3 pairs of each color combination. With right sides together, stitch the strips together along the long edges. Press the seams toward the

darker fabric. From each of the 3 strip-set color combinations, cut a total of 20 segments, each 2¾" wide (60 total).

Make 3 strip sets of each color combination. Cut 20 segments of each color combination (60 total).

4. Using pieces from the same color combination, arrange half-square-triangle units, two-patch segments, and an embroidered square together in rows as shown to make each block. Rotate the half-square-triangle units and two-patch segments to reflect the established block arrangement. Make 5 blocks from each color combination (15 total).

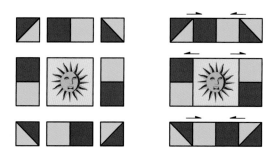

Make 5 from each color combination (15 total).

5. Refer to your worksheet grid to stitch the blocks into 5 horizontal rows of 3 blocks each. Stitch the rows together.

6. Referring to "Adding Borders" on pages 71–72, sew the inner border to the top and bottom of the quilt top and then to the sides, piecing as necessary. Press the seams toward the border. Repeat for the outer border.

Finishing the Quilt

Refer to "Quilt Finishing" on pages 71–78.

1. Layer the quilt top with batting and backing; baste.
2. Quilt as desired.
3. Bind the edges of the quilt.
4. Add a hanging sleeve and label if desired.

The embroidered motifs set the tone for the machine quilting. Different sizes and styles of stars in gold metallic thread continue the celestial theme. Spirals and loops were also added.

Island Star

Island Star: BEST OF THE NORTHWEST by M'Liss Rae Hawley,
2000, Freeland, Washington; quilted by Barbara Dau.

*I*n my desire to make the quilts in this second fat-quarter book a little more challenging, I decided that a star block seemed a natural. I wanted something not too small, not too big, and not too complicated! When I also decided not to use half-square-triangle units, the Island Star was born! It is an adaptable block that can take on many different looks depending on color placement.

Fat-Quarter Adviser

Each block requires 3 fat-quarter fabrics and the background fabric. Begin by dividing your fat-quarter packet in half by color value. Put 1 light, 1 medium, and 1 dark fat quarter in each half. You will make 6 blocks from each of the 2 color combinations.

In my quilt "Best of the Northwest," I selected the darkest fabrics for the longest point of the star, the lightest fabrics for the short point of the star, and the medium-color fabrics for the four-patch units. Remember, this is just a guide!

Finished Quilt: 61½" x 51½"
Finished Block: 10"

Materials

*All yardage is based on 42"-wide fabric
unless otherwise stated.*

¾ yd. for background
1 packet of 6 fat quarters for blocks
¼ yd. for inner border
¾ yd. for outer border
3¼ yds. for backing
⅝ yd. for binding
Crib-size batting (45" x 60")

Cutting

Cut along the 17" length of the fat quarters.

From the background fabric, cut:
6 strips, each 2¼" x 42". Crosscut to make 96 squares, each 2¼" x 2¼".

4 strips, each 2¼" x 42". Crosscut to make 8 strips, each 2¼" x 18".

From *each* of the 2 fat quarters for the long points of the star, cut:
8 strips, each 2¼" x 18". Crosscut to make 24 rectangles, each 2¼" x 5¾".

From *each* of the 2 fat quarters for the short points of the star, cut:
6 strips, each 2¼" x 18". Crosscut to make 24 rectangles, each 2¼" x 4".

2 squares, each 5½" x 5½", for outer-border corner squares.

From *each* of the two fat quarters for the four-patch units, cut:
4 strips, each 2¼" x 18"

From the inner-border fabric, cut:
4 strips, each 1¼" x 42"

From the outer-border fabric, cut:
4 strips, each 5½" x 42"

From the binding fabric, cut:
5 strips, each 3" x 42"

Assembling the Quilt Top

1. On the wrong side of each 2¼" background square, draw a diagonal line from corner to corner with the marking tool of your choice.

2. To make the long-star-point units, place a 2¼" background square on one end of each 2¼" x 5¾" fat-quarter rectangle as shown,

right sides together and raw edges aligned. Stitch directly on the diagonal line. Cut away the excess fabric, leaving a ¼" seam allowance. Press the seams toward the fat-quarter fabric. Make 24 of each color combination (48 total).

Make 24 of each
color combination
(48 total).

3. To make the short-star-point units, repeat step 2, placing a 2¼" background square on one end of each 2¼" x 4" fat-quarter rectangle as shown, right sides together and raw edges aligned. Make 24 of each color combination (48 total).

Make 24 of each
color combination
(48 total).

4. To make the four-patch units, with right sides together, stitch each 2¼" x 18" fat-quarter strip to a 2¼" x 18" background strip. Press the seams toward the darker fabric. Make 4 of each color combination. Cut 48 segments, each 2¼" wide, from each of the 2 strip-set color combinations (96 total).

2¼"

Make 4 strip sets of each color combination.
Cut 48 segments of each color combination (96 total).

5. Stitch 2 segments from the same color combination together as shown. Press the seam in one direction. Make 24 four-patch units of each color combination (48 total).

Make 24 of each
color combination
(48 total).

6. To make the blocks, follow the established color combinations to stitch a four-patch unit to a short-star-point unit. Press the seam allowance toward the short-star-point unit. Stitch a long-star-point unit to the bottom of the four-patch and short-star-point units. Press the seam toward the long-star-point unit. Make 24 of each color combination (48 total).

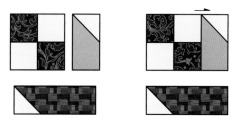

Make 24 of each
color combination
(48 total).

7. Stitch together 4 identical units from step 6, rotating the units as shown to complete the block. Make 6 of each color combination (12 total).

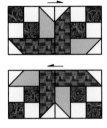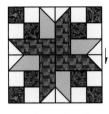

Make 6 of each color combination (12 total).

8. Stitch the blocks into 4 horizontal rows of 3 blocks each. Alternate the position of the 2 color combinations as shown below. Stitch the rows together.

9. Referring to "Adding Borders" on pages 71–72, sew the inner border to the top and bottom edges of the quilt top and then to the sides, piecing as necessary. Press the seams toward the border. Stitch the outer border to the top and bottom edges of the quilt top. Press the seams toward the outer border. Sew an outer-border corner square to each end of the two remaining border strips. Stitch the borders to the sides of the quilt top. Press the seams toward the outer border.

Finishing the Quilt

Refer to "Quilt Finishing" on pages 71–78.

1. Layer the quilt top with batting and backing; baste.
2. Quilt as desired.
3. Bind the edges of the quilt.
4. Add a hanging sleeve and label if desired.

Stippling fills the background fabric and arcs curve within each four patch. Stitched in variegated rayon thread, a swirling design enhances each star.

Longitude: GALACTIC LONGITUDE by M'Liss Rae Hawley, 2000, Freeland, Washington; quilted by Barbara Dau.

*L*ines of longitude run north to south, pole to pole. By international agreement, 0° longitude, also known as the prime meridian, runs through Greenwich, England. My quilt pattern Longitude is named after these imaginary lines that continue to guide mariners.

Longitude is a bright combination of strip-set segments, half-square-triangle blocks, and paper-pieced Nautical Flags blocks. The pieced border with corner squares adds something new to the mix but is not difficult to achieve. This is a festive little quilt that goes together quickly. It works great as a wall hanging or baby quilt. Have fun!

❖ ❖ ❖

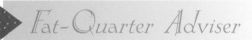

Begin with a theme: stars, chickens, nautical, or whatever you like. Many fat-quarter packets come grouped in this fashion. Label the fat quarters 1–6. You will use fat quarters 1–5 in the strip sets. You will use the dark print for a strip set, and the dark print, theme print, and fat quarter 6 for the half-square-triangle blocks and paper-pieced flags.

Finished Quilt: 37" x 46"
Finished Block: 3"

Materials

All yardage is based on 42"-wide fabric unless otherwise stated.

1 packet of 6 fat quarters for strip sets and
   blocks
⅝ yd. coordinating dark print for strip sets
   and blocks
¾ yd. coordinating theme print for blocks
¼ yd. light print for pieced border
⅝ yd. dark print for pieced border
1¾ yds. for backing
½ yd. for binding
Crib-size batting (45" x 60")
Foundation paper

Cutting

Cut along the 20" length of the fat quarters.

From *each* of fat quarters 1–3, cut:
3 strips, each 2" x 20"

From fat quarter 3, also cut:
4 squares, each 5½" x 5½"

From *each* of fat quarters 4 and 5, cut:
3 strips, each 3½" x 20"

From fat quarter 6, cut:
2 strips, each 3⅞" x 20". Crosscut to make 6 squares, each 3⅞" x 3⅞"; cut each square in half once diagonally to make 12 triangles.

4 strips, each 2¼" x 20"

From the coordinating dark print, cut:
3 strips, each 2" x 20"

3 strips, each 3⅞" x 20". Crosscut to make 12 squares, each 3⅞" x 3⅞"; cut each square in half once diagonally to make 24 triangles.

5 strips, each 2¼" x 20"

From the coordinating theme print, cut:
2 strips, each 3⅞" x 20". Crosscut to make 6 squares, each 3⅞" x 3⅞"; cut each square in half once diagonally to make 12 triangles.

5 strips, each 3¾" x 20"

From the light pieced-border fabric, cut:

2 strips, each 1½" x 27½"

2 strips, each 1½" x 36½"

From the dark pieced-border fabric, cut:

2 strips, each 4½" x 27½"

2 strips, each 4½" x 36½"

From the binding fabric, cut:

4 strips, each 3" x 42"

Assembling the Quilt Top

1. Stitch together the 2" x 20" strips from fat quarters 1–3 and the 2" x 20" strips of the coordinating dark print as shown to make strip set A. Press the seams in one direction. Make 3. Stitch together the 3½" x 20" strips from fat quarters 4 and 5 as shown to make strip set B. Press the seams in one direction. Make 3. Cut each strip set into 15 segments, each 3½" wide.

2. To make vertical rows 1, 5, and 9, stitch a strip set B segment to the end of a strip set A segment as shown. Make 9. Stitch 3 pieced strips together to complete the row. Press the seams in one direction. Make 3.

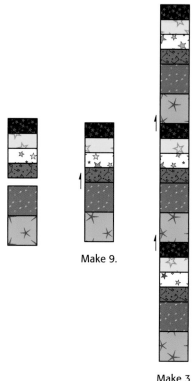

Make 9.

Make 3
(rows 1, 5, and 9).

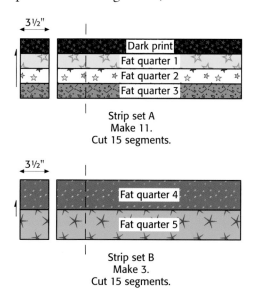

3½"

| Dark print |
| Fat quarter 1 |
| Fat quarter 2 |
| Fat quarter 3 |

Strip set A
Make 11.
Cut 15 segments.

3½"

| Fat quarter 4 |
| Fat quarter 5 |

Strip set B
Make 3.
Cut 15 segments.

3. To make vertical rows 3 and 7, stitch a strip set B segment to a strip set A segment as shown. Make 6. Stitch 3 pieced strips together to complete the row. Press the seams in one direction. Make 2.

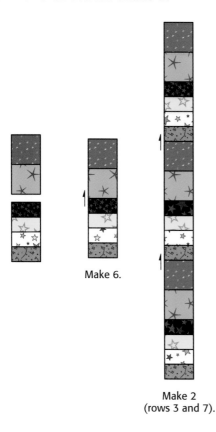

Make 6.

Make 2
(rows 3 and 7).

4. To make the half-square-triangle blocks, place a dark-print triangle on each fat quarter 6 and theme-print triangle, right sides together. Stitch the triangles together along the long edges. Press the seams toward the dark print. Make 12 of each color combination (24 total).

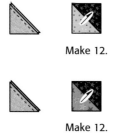

Make 12.

Make 12.

5. Referring to "Paper-Piecing Guidelines" on page 13, trace or photocopy the pattern below onto the foundation paper. Make 24 foundation patterns. Cut out the patterns along the outer edges.

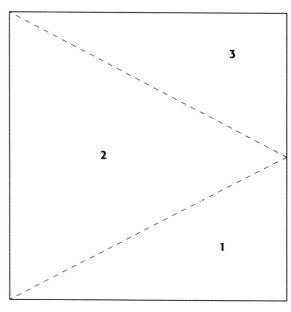

Longitude foundation pattern

6. With the marked side of the pattern face up, hold the pattern up to a light source and place the 2¼" x 20" strip from fat quarter 6 under the area marked 1. Place the wrong side of the fabric against the unmarked side of the pattern. Place the 3¾" x 20" theme-print strip over the 2¼" x 20" strip, right sides together. Be sure the edges of both strips extend ¼" beyond the seam line and ⅜" beyond the outer edges. Stitch on the line between areas 1 and 2.

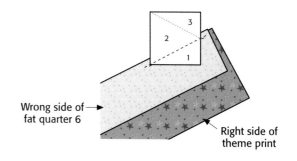

Wrong side of → fat quarter 6

Right side of theme print ←

7. Fold back the pattern along the seam line and trim the seam allowance to ¼". From the fabric side, fold up the theme-print strip and press it into place. It should cover area 2 and extend at least ¼" into area 3. From the pattern side, trim the excess fabric ⅜" from the pattern edges.

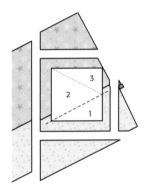

8. Place the 2¼" x 20" dark-print strip over the area 2 piece, right sides together. Stitch on the line between areas 2 and 3.

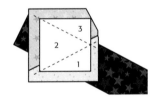

9. Refer to step 7 to trim the seam allowance and press the strip into place.

10. Trim the excess fabrics ¼" from the pattern edges. Make 24 paper-pieced blocks.

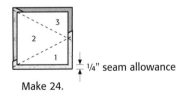

¼" seam allowance

Make 24.

11. To make rows 2 and 6, arrange the half-square-triangle blocks and paper-pieced blocks as shown. Press the seams in one direction. Make 2. To make rows 4 and 8, arrange the remaining half-square-triangle blocks and paper-pieced blocks as shown. Press the seams in one direction. Make 2.

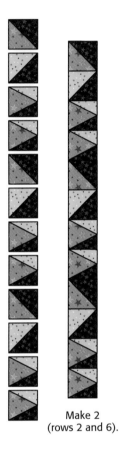

Make 2
(rows 2 and 6).

Make 2
(rows 4 and 8).

12. Join the rows vertically as shown.

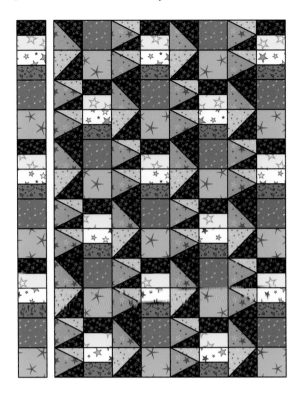

13. Staystitch along the edges of the 4 outside paper-pieced blocks. Remove the foundation paper from all of the paper-pieced blocks.

14. With right sides together, stitch together the 1½" x 27" light-print and 4½" x 27½" dark-print border strips along the long edges. Press the seams toward the dark-print strip. Repeat with the 36½" border strips.

Make 2 top- and bottom-border strips.

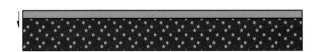

Make 2 side-border strips.

15. Referring to "Adding Borders" on pages 71–72, sew the pieced border to the top and bottom edges of the quilt top. Press the seams toward the border. Sew a 5½" border corner square to each end of the two remaining border strips. Stitch the borders to the sides of the quilt top. Press the seams toward the border.

Finishing the Quilt

Refer to "Quilt Finishing" on pages 71–78.

1. Layer the quilt top with batting and backing; baste.
2. Quilt as desired.
3. Bind the edges of the quilt.
4. Add a hanging sleeve and label if desired.

"Galactic Longitude" is made entirely of star-print fabrics. Stars and loops are quilted in variegated metallic thread along the vertical rows, while continuous loops fill the borders.

Prairie Queen

Prairie Queen: PRAIRIE FAIRIES by M'Liss Rae Hawley,
2000, Freeland, Washington; quilted by Barbara Dau.

Near my home on Whidbey Island there is a small historic land reserve named Ebey's Prairie. Suspended in time, the pristine landscape looks much as it did when the first European sea captains stepped ashore on the beach below. Prairie Queen is one of my favorite traditional blocks, and I stitch it in honor of Ebey's Prairie.

✧ ✧ ✧

Fat-Quarter Adviser

For this quilt, you will need 2 packets of fat quarters—1 packet of light fabrics for the background pieces and 1 packet of dark fabrics for the foreground pieces. You will also need yardage of an additional light fabric for the center squares. When selecting the light fabrics, it is best to choose fabrics from the same color family.

Before you begin cutting, pair each dark fat quarter with a light fat quarter. Each individual block will require two of the pairs: one pair for the four-patch units and one pair for the half-square-triangle units. Determine which pairs will be used together and label each pair with its intended use (four-patch or half-square-triangle units). Label the combinations 1–3. You will be making 12 blocks from each combination (36 total), but the quilt requires only 35 blocks. Use the remaining block to make a throw pillow or incorporate it into the backing if desired.

Finished Quilt: 59" x 75½"
Finished Block: 7½"

Materials

All yardage is based on 42"-wide fabric unless otherwise stated.

1 packet of 6 dark fat quarters for blocks
1 packet of 6 light fat quarters for block backgrounds
⅜ yd. coordinating light color for block centers
¾ yd. for sashing
⅜ yd. for inner border
1½ yds. for outer border and sashing corner squares
4¼ yds. for backing
¾ yd. for binding
Twin-size batting (72" x 90")
6" Bias Square ruler

Cutting

Cut along the 20" length of the fat quarters.

From *each* of the 6 fat quarters designated for four-patch units, cut:
    9 strips, each 1¾" x 20"

From the coordinating light color, cut:
    3 strips, each 3" x 42". Crosscut to make 36 squares, each 3" x 3".

From the sashing fabric, cut:
    17 strips, 1¼" x 42". Crosscut to make 82 strips, each 1¼" x 8".

From the inner-border fabric, cut:
    5 strips, each 2" x 42"

From the outer-border fabric, cut:
    6 strips, each 7½" x 42", for outer border

    2 strips, each 1¼" x 42". Crosscut to make 48 squares, each 1¼" x 1¼".

From the binding fabric, cut:
    7 strips, each 3" x 42"

Assembling the Quilt Top

1. To make the four-patch units, with right sides together, stitch each 1¾" x 20" light strip to a 1¾" x 20" dark strip along the long edges. Stitch the strips into color combinations as determined earlier. Press the seams toward the dark fabric. Make 9 strip sets of each color combination (27 total). Cut 96 segments, each 1¾" wide, from each of the 3 color combinations (288 total).

Make 9 strip sets of each color combination (27 total).
Cut 96 segments from each color combination (288 total).

2. Stitch 2 segments from the same color combination together as shown. Press the seam in one direction. Make 48 four-patch units of each color combination (144 total).

Make 48 of each
color combination
(144 total).

3. Using the fat quarters designated for half-square-triangle units, place each light fat quarter over its corresponding dark fat quarter, right sides up. Beginning at the corner of the fabric, place the rulers on the fabric as shown, with the long ruler at a 45°

angle. Cut along the right-hand edge of the long ruler. Using the first cut as a guide, cut 2¾"-wide strips across the entire piece.

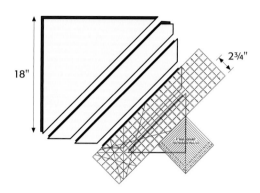

4. Separate the strips and rearrange them in order as shown, alternating the light and dark strips. You will have 2 sets of strips.

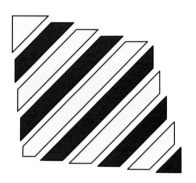

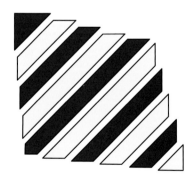

5. Sew the strips together along the long bias edge, right sides together. Offset the edges ¼" as shown. Press the seams toward the dark strips. The lower edge of the pieced rectangle and the adjacent side edge should be even after the strips are stitched together. The remaining 2 edges will be irregular.

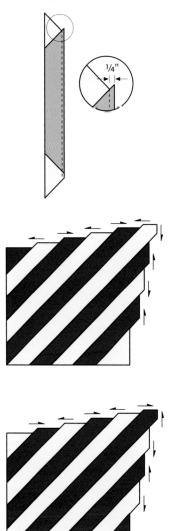

6. From each pair of pieced rectangles, use the Bias Square ruler to cut 48 half-square-triangle units. Begin cutting at the lower left corner of each rectangle. Align the 45° mark of the ruler on the seam line as shown to cut a square slightly larger than 3" x 3"; then cut along the side and top edges. After each square is cut, turn the square and

place the ruler on the opposite two sides and trim the square to 3" x 3".

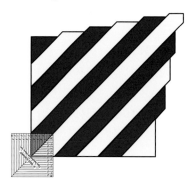

Align ruler's 45° mark on seam line

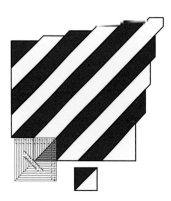

Cut first two sides of a square.

Cut final two sides.

7. Separate the half-square-triangle units and four-patch units into their designated color combinations. Sew 4 half-square-triangle units, 4 four-patch units, and 1 center square into blocks as shown. Make 12 blocks from each color combination (36 total).

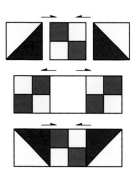

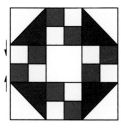

Make 12 from each color combination (36 total).

8. To make the block rows, alternately stitch 6 sashing strips and 5 blocks together as shown below, beginning and ending with a sashing strip. Press the seams toward the sashing strips.

9. To make the sashing rows, alternately stitch six 1¼" x 1¼" sashing corner squares and 5 sashing strips together as shown below, beginning and ending with a corner square. Press the seams toward the sashing strips. Make 8.

10. Stitch the rows together in order, alternating each block row with a sashing row. Press the seams toward the sashing rows.

11. Referring to "Adding Borders" on pages 71–72, sew the inner border to the top and bottom of the quilt top and then to the sides, piecing as necessary. Press the seams toward the border. Repeat for the outer border.

Finishing the Quilt

Refer to "Quilt Finishing" on pages 71–78.

1. Layer the quilt top with batting and backing; baste.
2. Quilt as desired.
3. Bind the edges of the quilt.
4. Add a hanging sleeve and label if desired.

Simple in-the-ditch quilting around sashing strips and corner stones contrasts with a dynamic, freehand "sea foam" design.

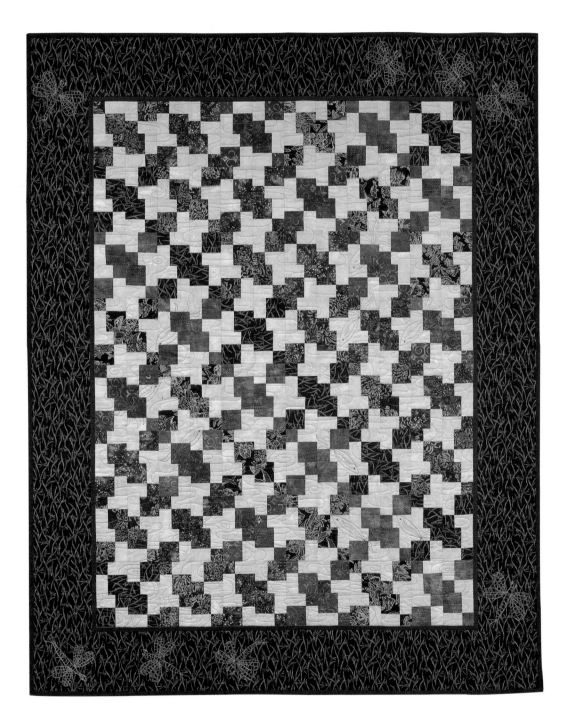

Strait of Georgia: TIDAL POOL by M'Liss Rae Hawley,
2000, Freeland, Washington; quilted by Barbara Dau.

A happy mistake, this pattern was discovered when a Prairie Queen four-patch went wrong! Now an original pattern, Strait of Georgia is one of my favorites.

Unsurpassed in its rugged beauty, the Strait of Georgia is a 150-mile channel between the mainland of British Columbia and Vancouver Island, Canada, and between Puget Sound and Queen Charlotte Sound. "Tidal Pool" is my under-the-sea interpretation of the Strait of Georgia quilt pattern.

"Joyous Women" (page 65) takes the same pattern in another direction. Six ethnic African fabrics are tied together with a mustard color background. In true African fashion, I used two different fabrics for the borders, cut them to different widths, and added two opposing corner squares. This quilt makes me smile!

Fat-Quarter Adviser

Any group of coordinating fabrics works well for this quilt. Pair the fat quarters with a light or dark background fabric and a coordinating border print, and you can't go wrong.

Finished Quilt: 51" x 64"
Finished Block: 6½"

Materials

All yardage is based on 42"-wide fabric unless otherwise stated.

1 packet of 6 fat quarters for blocks
1½ yds. for background
⅜ yd. for inner border
1 yd. for outer border
3¾ yds. for backing
⅝ yd. for binding
Twin-size batting (72" x 90")

Cutting

Cut along the 20" length of the fat quarters.

From *each* of the 6 fat quarters, cut:

    4 strips, each 2½" x 20"

    3 strips, each 1¾" x 20"

From the background fabric, cut:
    12 strips, each 1¾" x 42". Crosscut to make 24 strips, each 1¾" x 20".

    9 strips, each 2½" x 42". Crosscut to make 18 strips, each 2½" x 20".

From the inner-border fabric, cut:
    5 strips, each 1½" x 42"

From the outer-border fabric, cut:
    5 strips, each 5½" x 42"

From the binding fabric, cut:
    6 strips, each 3" x 42"

Assembling the Quilt Top

1. With right sides together, stitch each 2½" x 20" fat-quarter strip to a 1¾" x 20" background strip along the long edges. Make 4 of each color combination (24 total). Press the seams toward the fat-quarter strips. From each of the 6 color combinations, cut 32 segments, each 2½" wide (192 total).

Make 4 strip sets of each color combination (24 total).
Cut 32 segments of each color combination (192 total).

2. With right sides together, stitch each 1¾" x 20" fat-quarter strip to a 2½" x 20" background strip along the long edges. Make 3 of each color combination (18 total). Press the seams toward the fat-quarter strips. From each of the 6 color combinations, cut 32 segments, each 1¾" wide (192 total).

Make 3 strip sets of each color combination (18 total).
Cut 32 segments of each color combination (192 total).

3. Using segments from the same color combination, stitch a 2½" wide segment to a 1¾" wide segment. Make 32 of each color combination (192 total).

Make 32 of each
color combination
(192 total).

4. To make the blocks, stitch together 4 identical units from step 3, rotating the blocks as shown. Make 8 blocks of each color combination (48 total).

Make 8 of each
color combination
(48 total).

5. Stitch the blocks into 8 horizontal rows of 6 blocks each as shown. Stitch the rows together.

6. Referring to "Adding Borders" on pages 71–72, sew the inner border to the top and bottom of the quilt top and then to the sides, piecing as necessary. Press the seams toward the border. Repeat for the outer border.

Finishing the Quilt
Refer to "Quilt Finishing" on pages 71–78.

1. Layer the quilt top with batting and backing; baste.
2. Quilt as desired.
3. Bind the edges of the quilt.
4. Add a hanging sleeve and label if desired.

Triple Rail on Point: RISING SUN by M'Liss Rae Hawley,
2000, Freeland, Washington; quilted by Barbara Dau.

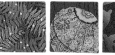

I think the Triple Rail is one of the most versatile blocks. Its sheer simplicity makes it a joy to work with. Placing the blocks on point makes for even more interesting quilts; they often look like weaving. Try a Triple Rail on Point with a color combination you have never used! Make a wall hanging or a baby quilt—it is fast and fun.

❖ ❖ ❖

Fat-Quarter Adviser

Color and value are the keys to this quilt. The design works best if you use 2 values each of 3 different coordinating colors. You may want to select the border fabric first and use it as a guide in selecting the block colors. You will also need a coordinating fabric for the corner and setting triangles.

Finished Quilt: 40" x 52"
Finished Block: 3"

Materials

All yardage is based on 42"-wide fabric unless otherwise stated.

1 packet of 6 fat quarters for blocks
⅝ yd. for background
¼ yd. for inner border
1⅛ yds. for outer border
3 yds. for backing
⅝ yd. for binding
Crib-size batting (45" x 60")

Cutting

Cut along the 20" length of the fat quarters.

From *each* fat quarter, cut:
   11 strips, each 1½" x 20"

From the background fabric, cut:
   2 strips, each 8" x 42". Crosscut to make 9 squares, each 8" x 8". Cut 2 squares in half once diagonally to make 4 half-square triangles for corner triangles; cut remaining 7 squares in half twice diagonally to make 28 quarter-square triangles for setting triangles.

From the inner-border fabric, cut:
   4 strips, each 1¼" x 42"

From the outer-border fabric, cut:
   6 strips, each 5¼" x 42"

From the binding fabric, cut:
   5 strips, each 3" x 42"

Assembling the Quilt Top

1. Separate the fat-quarter strips into 2 groups. Each group should contain the strips from 1 value of each of the 3 colors. Label the groups A and B.
2. To make strip set A, stitch together 1 strip of each color from group A along the long edges, right sides together. Press the seams in one direction. Make 11. Repeat for the group B strips, keeping the colors in the same positions as in strip set A. Make 11.

Crosscut each of the 2 strip-set groups to make 55 segments, each 3½" wide.

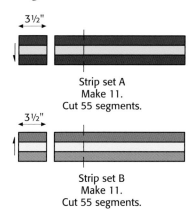

Strip set A
Make 11.
Cut 55 segments.

Strip set B
Make 11.
Cut 55 segments.

3. Stitch the blocks into 14 diagonal rows as shown below, alternating the block positions in each row. Press the seams of each row in the opposite direction of the previous row. Sew a quarter-square setting triangle to the ends of each row, keeping the straight-grain edge of each triangle along the quilt outer edges. The setting triangles are larger than necessary; you will trim them later. Press the seams toward the setting triangles.

4. Stitch the rows together. Press the seams in one direction. Sew a half-square corner triangle to each corner. The corner triangles are larger than necessary; you will trim them later. Press the seams toward the corner triangles.

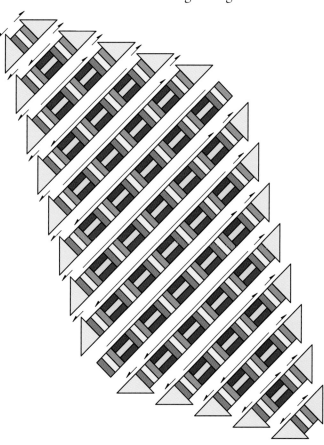

5. Square up the quilt top, using the points of the blocks as your guide for trimming the excess fabric from the setting and corner triangles.

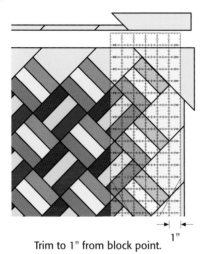

Trim to 1" from block point.

6. Referring to "Adding Borders" on pages 71–72, sew the inner border to the top and bottom of the quilt top and then to the sides, piecing as necessary. Press the seams toward the border. Repeat for the outer border.

Finishing the Quilt

Refer to "Quilt Finishing" on pages 71–78.

1. Layer the quilt top with batting and backing; baste.
2. Quilt as desired.
3. Bind the edges of the quilt.
4. Add a hanging sleeve and label if desired.

The Japanese fabric in "Rising Sun" set the quilt's theme. The quilting is a stylized Japanese wave pattern that is often used in embroidery.

Z Star: ADRIENNE'S AMETHYST, #16 by M'Liss Rae Hawley, 2000,
Freeland, Washington; quilted by M'Liss Rae Hawley and Barbara Dau.

*T*he Z Star began on paper as paper-pieced Zs. From conception to finished blocks on the quilt wall, the Zs did not make it as letters, but they looked really great as stars. So, you might end up with stars or Zs or something else altogether original! Whatever the end result, you are going to love it.

✧ ✧ ✧

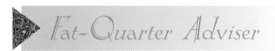

This design works best if you select a fat-quarter packet with 2 light prints, 2 medium prints, and 2 dark prints. You will also need 2 additional light fat quarters from a single color family for the background. Use the same color family and/or value in the paper piecing areas from block to block—purple and/or dark in each area 1, for example—to maintain the integrity of the pattern.

Finished Quilt: 28" x 38"
Finished Block: 5"

Materials

All yardage is based on 42"-wide fabric unless otherwise stated.

1 packet of 6 fat quarters for blocks
2 fat quarters from a single color family for background
½ yd. for border
1 yd. for backing
⅜ yd. for binding
Crib-size batting (45" x 60")
Foundation paper

Cutting

Cut along the 20" length of the fat quarters.

From *each* of the 8 fat quarters, cut:
5 strips, each 3¼" x 20"

From the border fabric, cut:
3 strips, each 4½" x 42"

From the binding fabric, cut:
4 strips, each 3" x 42"

Assembling the Quilt Top

1. Referring to "Paper-Piecing Guidelines" on page 13, trace or photocopy the patterns on page 50 onto the foundation paper. Make 24 A-unit foundation patterns and 4 B-unit foundation patterns. Cut out the patterns along the outer edges.

2. Make the A units. With the marked side of the pattern face up, hold the pattern up to a light source and place a background strip under the area on the pattern marked 1. Place the wrong side of the fabric against the unmarked side of the pattern. Place a medium-print fat-quarter strip over the background strip, right sides together. Be sure the edges of both strips extend ¼" beyond the solid line that runs between areas 1 and 2 and ⅜" beyond the outer edges. Stitch on the line between areas 1 and 2.

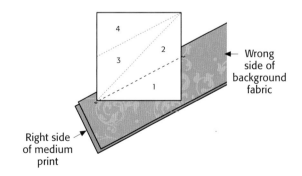

Wrong side of background fabric

Right side of medium print

3. Fold back the pattern along the seam line and trim the seam allowance to ¼". From the fabric side, fold up the medium-print strip and press it into place. It should cover area 2 and extend at least ¼" into area 3. From the pattern side, trim the excess fabric ⅜" from the pattern edges.

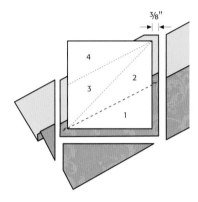

4. Continue in this manner, using a dark-print fat-quarter strip for area 3 and a light-print fat-quarter strip for area 4. Trim the excess fabrics ¼" from the pattern edges. Make 11 more A units with the same fabrics you used in the first. Make 12 A units with the other light, medium, dark, and background fat-quarter fabrics.

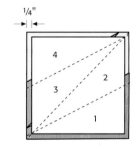

A unit
Make 12 from
first color group.

A unit
Make 12 from
second color group.

5. Make the B units in the same manner as the A units, making 2 in each of the 2 color combinations. Use a medium-print fat-quarter strip for area 1, a background strip for area 2, a dark-print fat-quarter strip for area 3, and a light-print fat-quarter strip for area 4.

B unit
Make 2 from
first color group.

B unit
Make 2 from
second color group.

6. Stitch together 4 A units, 2 from each color combination, as shown. Press the seams open. Make 6.

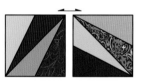

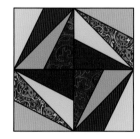

Make 6.

7. Stitch the blocks into 3 horizontal rows of 2 blocks each. Arrange the blocks the same way in each row. Press the seams open.

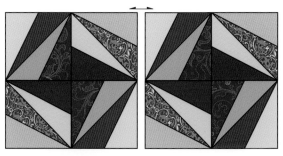

8. Staystitch around the edges of the quilt top. Carefully remove the paper foundations from the back of the quilt top.
9. Referring to "Adding Borders" on pages 71–72, sew the border to the top and bottom edges of the quilt top. Press the seams toward the border. Sew a foundation-pieced B unit to each end of the 2 remaining border strips, with identical blocks in opposing corners. Stitch the borders to the sides of the quilt top. Press the seams toward the border.

10. Staystitch the edges of the border foundation blocks. Carefully remove the paper foundations from the blocks.

Finishing the Quilt
Refer to "Quilt Finishing" on pages 71–78.

1. Layer the quilt top with batting and backing; baste.
2. Quilt as desired.
3. Bind the edges of the quilt.
4. Add a hanging sleeve and label if desired.

Quilting for "Adrienne's Amethyst, #16" includes stippling and outline quilting with Sliver metallic thread. Tied threads in the star centers add interest.

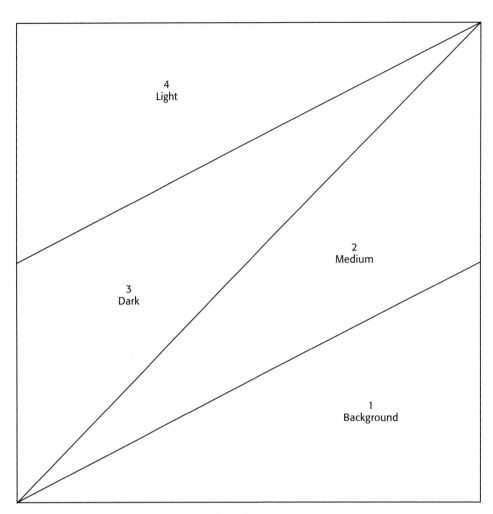

A-unit foundation pattern

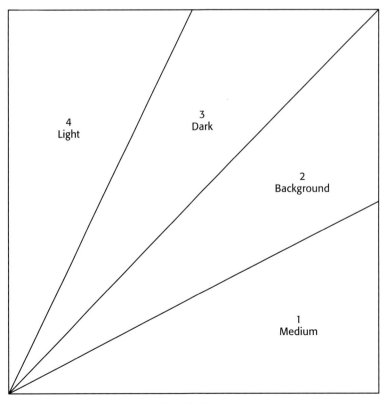

B-unit foundation pattern

Gallery of Quilts

✧ ✧ ✧ ✧

Bargello: OCEAN BEAUTY by Suzanne Y. Kincy, 2000,
Oak Harbor, Washington, 62" x 57"; quilted by Barbara Dau.

Instructions begin on page 14.

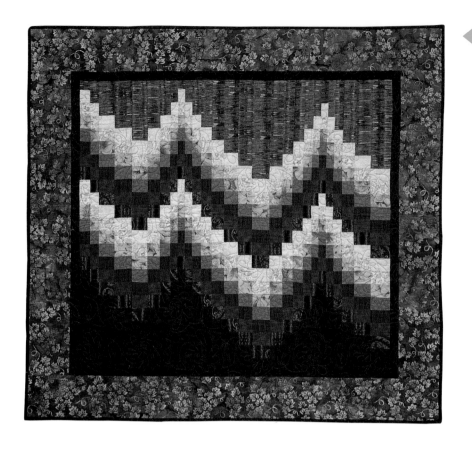

◀ **Bargello:** Fuschia Fantasy
by Beverly K. Green, 2000,
Port Townsend, Washington,
60" x 54"; quilted by
Rainshadow Quilting.

Instructions begin on page 14.

Bargello:
Winter Wonderland
by Vicky DeGraaf, 2001,
Langley, Washington,
60" x 54"; quilted by
Barbara Dau.

Instructions begin on page 14. ▶

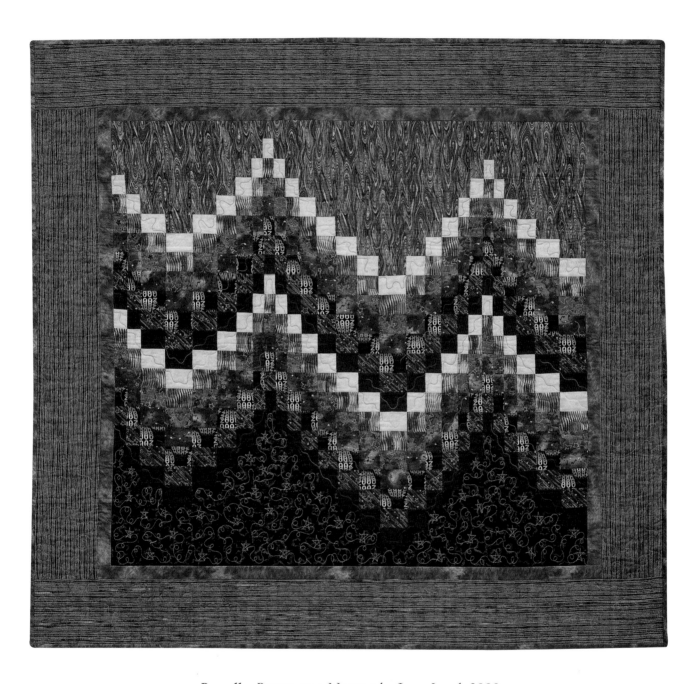

Bargello: BIRTH OF A NEBULA by Joyce Lund, 2000,
Lopez Island, Washington, 60" x 54"; quilted by Barbara Dau.
Instructions begin on page 14.

Embroidery Block: Outdoorsman by M'Liss Rae Hawley,
1999, Freeland, Washington, 39" x 57".

Instructions begin on page 19.

Embroidery Block:
MARINER'S EXCURSION
by Erin Rae Frandsen, 1999,
Mukilteo, Washington, 49" x 49";
quilted by Barbara Dau.

Instructions begin on page 19.

Embroidery Block:
VALENTINES FOR MICHAEL
by M'Liss Rae Hawley, 1999,
Freeland, Washington, 49" x 49";
quilted by Randy Silvers.

Instructions begin on page 19.

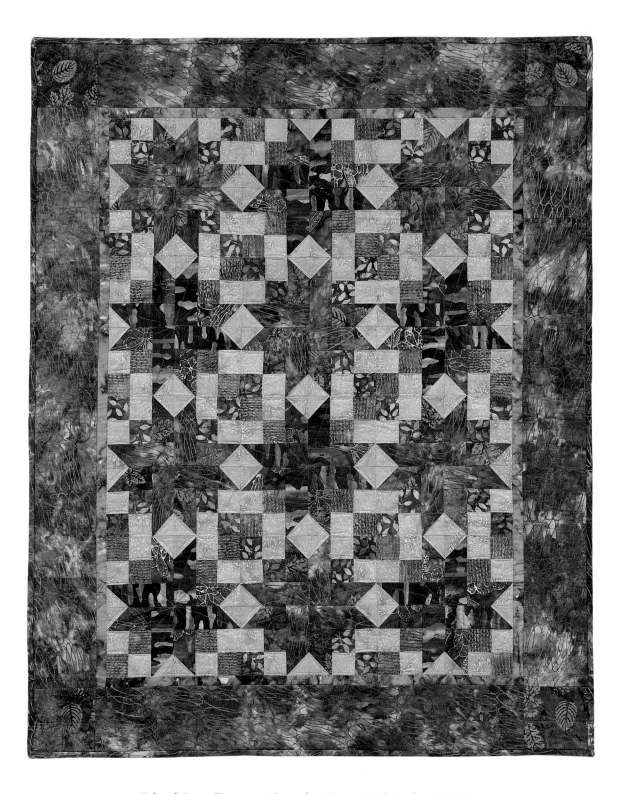

Island Star: EVENING STAR by Anastasia Riordan, 2000,
Langley, Washington, 41" x 51"; quilted by Barbara Dau.

Instructions begin on page 24.

◀ **Island Star:** WELL, IT STRIKES ME PINK
by Carol Chapman, 2000, Anacortes,
Washington, 41" x 51"; quilted by Jill Foss.

Instructions begin on page 24.

Island Star: A WHIDBEY FOURTH OF JULY ▶
by Peggy J. Johnson, 2000,
Langley, Washington, 41" x 51";
quilted by Barbara Dau.

Instructions begin on page 24.

Longitude: MEMORIES OF BRITEX,
LATITUDE 37, LONGITUDE 122
by M'Liss Rae Hawley, 2001,
Freeland, Washington, 37" x 46".

Instructions begin on page 28.

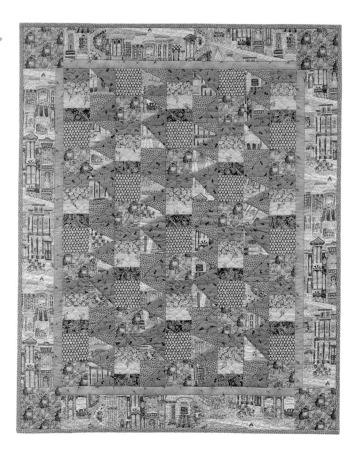

Longitude: MY FUNKY
ATTITUDE LATITUDE
by Peggy J. Johnson, 2001,
Langley, Washington, 37" x 46";
quilted by Barbara Dau.

Instructions begin on page 28.

Longitude: Nautical Magic by Dawn L. Lease,
2000, Lopez Island, Washington, 37" x 46".

Instructions begin on page 28.

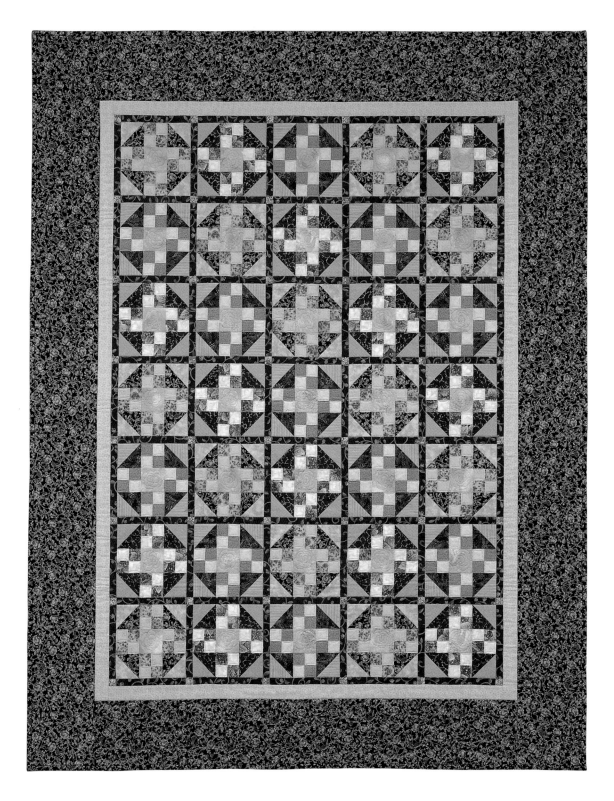

Prairie Queen: LAVENDER AND ROSES by Suzanne Y. Kincy, 2000,
Oak Harbor, Washington, 59" x 75½"; quilted by Barbara Dau.
Instructions begin on page 34.

Prairie Queen: FAIRY FROLIC
by Anastasia Riordan, 2000,
Langley, Washington, 59" x 75½";
quilted by Barbara Dau.

Instructions begin on page 34.

Prairie Queen: AN OLD PRAIRIE QUEEN
by Vicki DeGraaf, 2000,
Langley, Washington, 59" x 75½";
quilted by Barbara Dau.

Instructions begin on page 34.

Prairie Queen: "Hey Red! You Sure Are Looking Good!"
by Carla Zimmermann, 2001, Anacortes, Washington,
60" x 76"; quilted by Laverne S. Campbell.

Instructions begin on page 34.

Strait of Georgia: THE BIRDS FLEW OVER THE STRAIT by Annette M. Barca, 2000, Lynnwood, Washington, 54" x 66"; quilted by Barbara Dau.

Instructions begin on page 39.

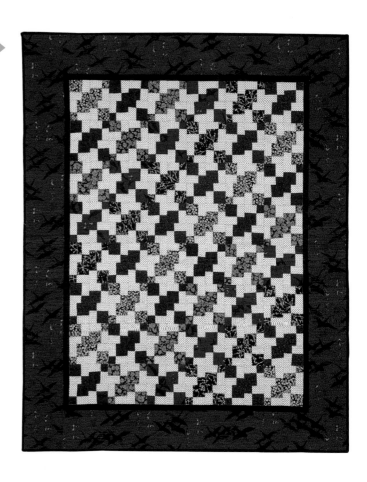

Strait of Georgia: DANCE OF THE DRAGONFLY by Leslie Rommann, 2000, Oak Harbor, Washington, 53" x 64"; quilted by Diane Brandt-Raines.

Instructions begin on page 39.

Strait of Georgia: GARDEN PATHS
by Suzanne Y. Kincy, 2000,
Oak Harbor, Washington, 54" x 66";
quilted by Barbara Dau.

Instructions begin on page 39.

Strait of Georgia:
AQUINNAH
by Joyce Lund, 2000,
Lopez Island, Washington,
52" x 64"; quilted by Barbara Dau.

Instructions begin on page 39.

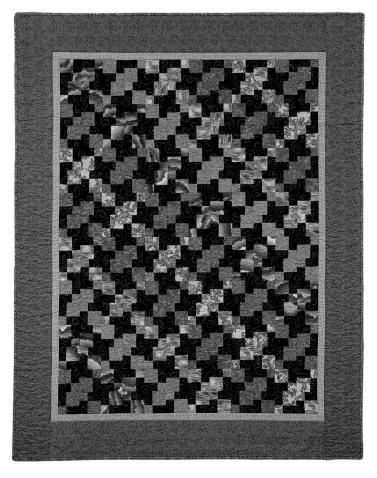

Strait of Georgia: Joyous Women by M'Liss Rae Hawley, 2000,
Freeland, Washington, 52" x 66"; quilted by Barbara Dau.
The African-made border fabric inspired this quilt's festive title.

Instructions begin on page 39.

Triple Rail on Point: KATZ N' JAMMERS
by Anastasia Riordan, 2000, Langley,
Washington, 40" x 53"; quilted by Barbara Dau.

Instructions begin on page 42.

Triple Rail on Point:
WASHINGTON GOLD
by Joni C. Cartwright, 2000,
Freeland, Washington,
54" x 41"; quilted by
Barbara Dau.

Instructions begin on page 42.

Triple Rail on Point: POLLY GONE WILD by Annette M. Barca, 2000,
Lynnwood, Washington, 43" x 55"; quilted by Barbara Dau.
Instructions begin on page 42.

Z Star: BLUE ICE by Dayle Gray, 2000,
Freeland, Washington, 28" x 38".

Instructions begin on page 46.

◀ **Z Star:** CHRISTMAS STAR
by M'Liss Rae Hawley, 2000,
Freeland, Washington,
28" x 38".

Instructions begin on page 46.

Z Star: ZEE HALLOWEEN QUILT ▶
by Annette M. Barca, 2000,
Lynnwood, Washington,
37½" x 43"; quilted by
Barbara Dau.

Instructions begin on page 46.

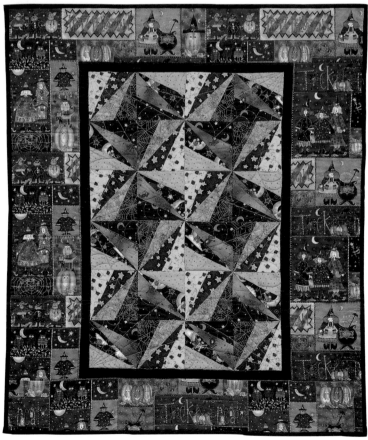

Island Star: FANTASY ISLAND by M'Liss Rae Hawley, 2001, Freeland, Washington, 42¼" x 52¾".

Instructions begin on page 24.

Quilt Finishing

✧ ✧ ✧ ✧ ✧

Adding Borders

The quilts in this book feature borders with either straight-cut corners or borders with corner squares. Most of the instructions call for the border strips to be cut across the width of the fabric. Because many of the border lengths are longer than the width of the fabric, some of the borders need to be pieced. To piece border strips, sew them together end to end and then trim to the required lengths. If you prefer to center the seam of a pieced border at the edge of the quilt top, you will need to cut two border strips for every side that is longer than the width of your fabric. This will require extra yardage. If you prefer unpieced borders, you will need to purchase enough fabric to cut full-length strips along the lengthwise grain of the border fabric.

Borders with Straight-Cut Corners

1. Measure the width of the quilt top through the horizontal center. Cut 2 border strips to this measurement, piecing and trimming strips as necessary to achieve the required length. Mark the centers of the border strips and the top and bottom edges of the quilt top.

2. With right sides together, pin the border strips to the top and bottom edges of the quilt top, matching center marks and ends. Stitch the borders in place, easing in any excess fabric as needed. Press the seams toward the border strips.

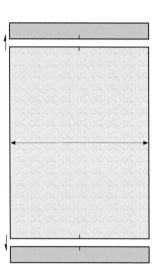

✧ Tip ✧

If the quilt top and border strips are not exactly the same length, layer the pieces so the longer piece is on the bottom when stitching. The sewing machine's feed dogs will help ease in the extra length.

3. Measure the length of the quilt top through the vertical center, including the top and bottom borders. Cut 2 border strips to this measurement, piecing and trimming strips as necessary to achieve the required length. Mark the center of the border strips and the sides of the quilt top.

4. With right sides together, pin the border strips to the sides of the quilt top, matching center marks and ends. Stitch the borders in place, easing in any excess fabric as needed. Press the seams toward the border strips.

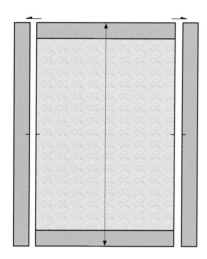

Borders with Corner Squares

1. Measure the width and length of your quilt top through the vertical and horizontal centers. Cut the border strips to these measurements, piecing and trimming strips as necessary to achieve the required length. Mark the center of the border strips and quilt-top edges.

2. With right sides together, pin the top and bottom border strips to the top and bottom edges of the quilt top, matching center marks and ends. Stitch the borders in place, easing in any excess fabric as needed. Press the seams toward the border strips.

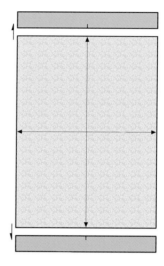

3. Sew a corner square to each end of the side border strips. Press the seams toward the border strips. Pin the border strips to the sides of the quilt top, matching center marks and ends. Stitch the borders in place, easing in any excess fabric as needed. Press the seams toward the border strips.

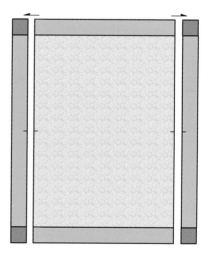

Choosing Batting

There are many different types of batting, and new ones are always being introduced, so how do you decide which one to use? First, determine whether you will be hand or machine quilting the project. Some battings are more suitable for hand quilting because they are easier to needle, while others handle better when machine quilting. I machine quilt most of my tops, and I find that a cotton batting works best. My batting of choice is Quilter's Dream Cotton, which is available in four weights and six sizes.

The project's end use should also be a factor when selecting a batting. Are you using the batting as a wall hanging, a bed quilt, or a garment? Battings that drape well are preferable for bed quilts and garments, while a stiffer batting is good for wall hangings. If you need warmth, such as for a bed quilt or jacket, consider a polyester or wool batting.

Consider, also, how the project will be cleaned. An easy-care batting such as polyester is a good choice for bed quilts and garments that may be washed frequently.

You may have already developed your own batting preferences, but if not, hand and machine quilt a few samples. Use a variety of battings sandwiched between a top and bottom fabric to determine which batting handles best and gives you the desired look and feel.

Layering and Basting

Before the project can be quilted, you must layer the quilt top, batting, and backing and temporarily join the layers together with basting. It is critical that you join the layers correctly in this step; any wrinkles or folds will be emphasized when you quilt the project. To help make the process easier and more accurate, assemble the layers on a work surface large enough to accommodate the entire project.

1. Press the quilt top from the back—this is the last opportunity to set the seams in the correct direction. Once your seams are set, press from the front. Use spray starch or sizing if desired.

2. Cut the backing and batting about 4" larger than the quilt top on all sides.

3. Press the backing fabric. Use spray starch or sizing if desired.

4. Lay the backing, right side down, on a clean, flat surface. Secure it with masking tape in several places along the edges. The fabric should be taut but not stretched. Lay the batting on the backing; secure with masking tape. Place the quilt top, right side up, over the batting; secure with masking tape.

5. Beginning in the center of the quilt top and working toward the center of the quilt's outer top edge, hand baste the layers together. Return to the center, basting to the quilt's outer bottom edge. Continue basting vertically, spacing the rows about 4" apart. Repeat the process to baste the

horizontal rows and then the 2 diagonal rows. Complete the basting process by basting around the entire outer edge. I prefer hand basting with thread to pin basting because it allows me to machine quilt without stopping to remove pins.

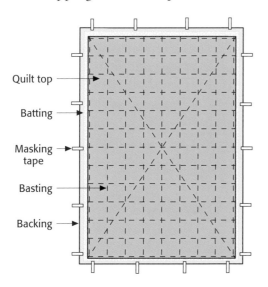

Quilt top
Batting
Masking tape
Basting
Backing

6. After basting the quilt, remove the tape. You are now ready to quilt!

Quilting

The quilt designs in this book offer an array of quilting possibilities. For example, the Bargello quilts on page 14 and pages 51–53 provide wonderful spaces for showcasing machine or hand quilting. In one of these quilts, "Bow Wow Chow Mein" (page 14), I made templates of individual scenes from the border fabric, along with a dachshund and other dog articles, and had my machine quilter, Barbara Dau, translate them to the quilt. For the Embroidery Block quilts (page 19 and pages 54–55), stitching in the ditch worked well for "Outdoorsman" (page 54), while an overall horizontal quilting design was used for "Valentines for Michael" (page 55).

I usually machine quilt small projects myself and have larger quilts professionally quilted. Sometimes I have only part of a quilt professionally quilted and do the remainder myself. You may want to use a combination of machine quilting and hand quilting. Combining a variety of techniques and threads can be very effective. Consult with a professional quilter if you need suggestions on what quilting design or thread color to use.

Ultimately, you are the best judge of the quilting that will complement your work. I enjoy designing machine-quilting patterns as I quilt; it allows me freedom and flexibility as I move around a quilt top.

Squaring Up a Quilt

When you have completed the quilting, you will need to square up your quilt. This means cutting off the excess backing and batting, as well as cleaning up any threads or uneven sections of border.

Align a ruler with the seam of the outer border and measure to the edge of the quilt in a number of places. Use the narrowest measurement as a guide for positioning your ruler and trimming the excess all around the quilt.

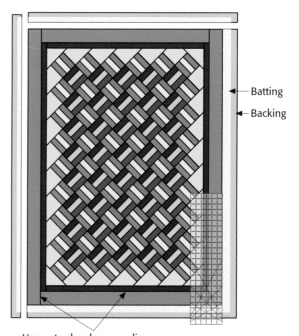

Batting
Backing

Use outer-border seam lines as a guide for squaring up the quilt.

Next, fold the quilt in half, and then fold it again in the other direction. Does your quilt have square corners and edges that are equal in length? If not, this is your last chance to correct them. Use a large, square ruler to square up the corners.

Use a basting or serpentine stitch around the edge to stabilize the quilt—do not use a zigzag stitch. Once you have squared-up your quilt top, you are ready for the finishing touches: the binding, hanging sleeve, and label.

Binding

The construction of your binding is very important. Working as a judge in quilt competitions has made this abundantly clear to me. Participants do not always take care with their bindings, and a poorly made binding can make an otherwise lovely quilt look sloppy. The following binding method combines the best of detail, strength, and beauty.

1. Cut enough 3"-wide binding strips to equal the perimeter of the quilt plus 10" for seams and corners. Cut the strips across the width of the fabric. I cut strips on the bias only if I want to take advantage of a diagonal print or if I need to fit the binding around rounded corners.

2. Join the strips at right angles as shown to make one long continuous strip. Trim the seam allowances to ¼" and press the seams open.

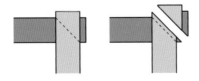

3. Press the binding in half lengthwise, wrong sides together.

4. With raw edges even, lay the binding on the quilt top, 6" from the upper left-hand corner. Using a ½"-wide seam allowance, begin stitching 4" from the end of the binding (10" from the corner).

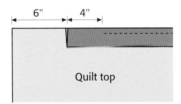

5. Stitch about 2", stop, and cut the threads. Remove the quilt from the machine and fold the binding to the back; it should barely cover the stitching line you just made. If the binding overlaps the stitching line too much, stitch again, just inside the first stitching line. If the binding doesn't cover the original stitching, stitch just outside the original stitching. Remove the extra stitches before you proceed.

6. Using the stitching position you determined in step 5, stitch to within ½" of the first corner. Stop, backstitch, cut the thread, and remove the quilt from the machine.

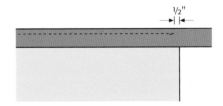

7. Fold the binding up to create a 45° angle. Holding the folded edge in place, fold the binding down, aligning the new fold with the top edge of the quilt and the raw edge with the side of the quilt. Beginning at the top edge, stitch the binding to the quilt, stopping ½" from the next corner. Repeat the folding and stitching process for the remaining corners.

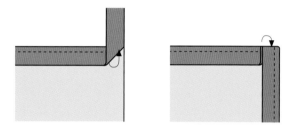

8. After turning the last corner, stitch about 3"; backstitch, and remove the quilt from the machine. Cut the ending tail of the binding so it overlaps the beginning tail of the binding 3".

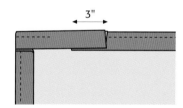

9. Lay the quilt so the top is right side up. Unfold the unstitched ends of the binding tails. Pin the tails right sides together at right angles. Draw a line from the upper left-hand corner to the lower right-hand corner of the binding. Stitch along this line.

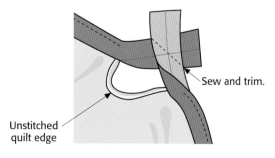

Sew and trim.

Unstitched quilt edge

10. Check to make sure the binding is the correct length to cover the unbound edge of the quilt. Carefully trim the seam allowance to ¼". Press the seam open. Re-press the binding in half. Finish stitching the binding to the quilt.

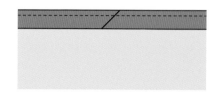

11. Fold the binding to the back of the quilt and pin it in place. I pin approximately 12" at a time. Hand stitch the binding to the quilt back, matching the thread to the binding and carefully mitering the corners as you approach them. Hand stitch each side of the mitered corners.

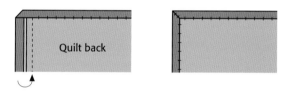

Quilt back

Adding a Hanging Sleeve

If you want to display your quilt on a wall, you need to add a sleeve to protect your work of art from undue strain.

1. Cut a 7½"-wide strip of backing fabric across the width of the fabric (if the quilt is wider than 40", cut 2 strips and stitch them together, end to end). Cut the strip 1" shorter than the width of your quilt. Press the short ends under ¼" and stitch them in place.

2. Fold the sleeve in half lengthwise, right sides together. Stitch the raw edges together; press. Turn the sleeve right side out and press again.

3. Mark the center of the top edge of the quilt and the center of the long, folded edge of the sleeve. With the center marks aligned, pin the sleeve to the quilt back, placing the folded edge of the sleeve next to the binding. Blindstitch the folded edge in place.

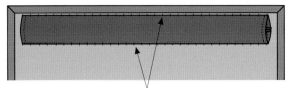

Blindstitch top and bottom of sleeve to quilt.

4. Push up the bottom edge of the sleeve just a bit to provide a little give so the hanging rod does not put strain on the quilt. Blindstitch the lower edge of the sleeve in place, being careful not to stitch through to the front of the quilt.

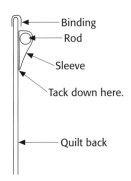

Binding
Rod
Sleeve
Tack down here.
Quilt back

Making a Label

Labels provide important information about you and your quilt. I make my labels about 4" x 7" so that I have plenty of room. Your labels should include at least the following information:

✦ The name of the quilt

✦ Your full name

✦ Your business name, if applicable

✦ Your city, county, state or province, and country of residence

✦ The date

✦ Who you made the quilt for if you made it for a specific person, or why you made the quilt if you made it for a particular event

You may also wish to add the following information to the label:

✦ What series the quilt belongs to, if applicable

✦ A quilting teacher's name, if applicable

✦ A story connected with the piece, especially one close to your heart

There are many ways to make a label. If your sewing machine has a lettering system, use it. If you own or have access to an embroidery machine, use it. Embroidery machines offer wonderful opportunities for embellishing your label. You may even want to create your own logo.

Other label-making methods include drawing and writing with permanent fabric markers and using photo-transfer techniques. If you use permanent markers, be sure to back the label with freezer paper, stabilizer, or interfacing while you letter it.

You may also want to include embroidered patches, decals, buttons, ribbons, or lace. Simply stitch them to the label to make it as unique as you are. I also like to include leftover blocks to link the quilt top to the back.

When is the correct time to attach your label? You can sew it to the lower right corner of the quilt back before the quilt is basted or quilted. Or, you can hand stitch your label to the quilt backing after the quilting is complete.